Dice Games for Kids

38 Brilliant Dice Games to Enjoy at School or at Home

***

Lindsay Small

Creator of
www.ActivityVillage.co.uk
Keeping Kids Busy

For David, Josh and Tilly, who helped test these games over the years

Table of Contents

Introduction

Dice games are fun! They are also one of the oldest of all kinds of games, with records of dice being played over 5,000 years ago. Dice have been found in Egyptian tombs and were very popular in Roman times.

Dice games are versatile! They can be based on luck, or on skill and planning. You can find games to play with two players or twenty, on the floor with 3-year olds and on a table with 70-year olds.

Dice games are educational! They are educational in obvious ways, encouraging counting and numbers in little children and quick mental addition in older children. But they are also excellent at reinforcing the concept of taking turns, scoring (both mental and on paper), winning and losing gracefully, patience and so much more.

Dice games are portable! You can always find room for a few dice in the bottom of a handbag or pocket, and most games require no more than a paper and pencil to go with them. Or you can "pre-package" some of your favourite games in a little bag or box and include it easily in an overnight case for traveling.

Dice are cheap! You probably have a number of interesting dice lurking in existing family games, and you can certainly pick up more very cheaply these days through stationery shops, discount stores, gaming shops, educational catalogues or garage sales. I have been known to buy an old board game for pennies from a charity shop just to acquire its dice!

Dice are collectible! There are so many different kinds of dice to choose from now readily available in the shops or by mail order. Most children love the look and feel of dice and are happy to build up a collection - and are likely to choose a few particular dice to be their favourites, too. Build up your store and keep them in their own box with a stack of counters and favourite playing pieces and perhaps a shaker or two.

Adapting Dice

You can easily adapt existing dice with stickers if you can't find just what you are looking for, or make your own dice from scratch with blanks (available from educational suppliers). Cover each surface with clear contact paper for more permanence, or add a light coat of varnish. Wooden cubes (find them at craft stores) can also be used.

Containers for dice: If you use your imagination and keep your eyes open you can find all sorts of fun containers for your dice collection. Small plastic sweet containers (some come in bright plastic tubes with attached lids), film canisters, potato crisp cans, spice containers, washing tablet bags, drawstring bags, little boxes, re-sealable plastic bags, and pencil cases are just a few examples.

Shakers and dice cups: Sometimes using a shaker can be fun. You could buy the traditional leather shakers, which wear wonderfully with age - but plastic cups and mugs, empty potato crisp cans and even an empty yoghurt tub can make good alternatives.

Noise control: Felt makes a great surface for dice games and can easily be folded, stored and carried around. Craft foam also works well but needs to be rolled for storage. For home use you could line an old wooden tray with felt or craft foam – perfect to help younger children keep dice on the table! In the classroom you could hand out the lids of shoe-boxes so that each child can roll the dice on the table in front of them.

Traveling dice: Use a small box or plastic tub: cut out a hole in the top and line it with a see-through piece of plastic or acrylic. Throw in some dice, attach the top (using elastic bands if necessary) and you have a perfect traveling container. It's good for preventing cheating too!

A Note about Extra Equipment

I've tried to keep the extra equipment you will need to the minimum, but the games in this section, aimed at younger children, may call for some preparation. You may have to gather together some small toys or counters, colouring pencils and stickers, and draw a quick homemade "game board".

You can find ready-made printable versions for many of the game boards at ActvityVillage.co.uk/dice-games.

Some of these games also require that you adapt normal dice with small stickers.

Farmyard

The more hands-on practice young children have with counting, the easier it becomes to visualise numbers and give meaning to them. If you don't have farm animals, use counters, dinosaurs, cars, or anything else you have to hand. You will need to "doctor" a die and create a very simple playing board.

Age guide: 3+

Skills: Number recognition, one to one correspondence, counting, fine motor skills

Equipment: 1 die, on which you have replaced the sides with stickers showing the numbers 1, 2 and 3 twice. Plastic farm animals or similar small objects. There is a printable version of this game board at ActivityVillage.co.uk/farmyard.

To play: You will need one "game board" for each player, and lots of farm animals. For a farmyard game board you simply need a piece of green card, paper or craft foam onto which you have drawn 10 circles.

Put the animals in the centre of the table where all the children can reach them. The youngest child starts by rolling the die and selecting the appropriate number of animals to go into his field. The first child to place 10 wins. Encourage lots of counting along the way and ask plenty of questions ("How many more animals will Mary need to get to 10?")

Variations:

Number the circles 1-10. Place the animals on the board in the correct order.

Older children can be encouraged to roll the correct number to reach 10 exactly.

Turn the game round and start with 10 animals in the field. The first to take all the animals away is the winner.

Play with cars and "park your cars in the garage".

Teddy Bear, Teddy Bear

Teddy Bear, Teddy Bear is an ideal introduction to dice games for very young children. They can learn to count the dots on the die and begin to recognise the patterns on the die by looking for the matching pattern on the teddies.

Age guide: 3+

Skills: Number recognition, one to one correspondence, counting, fine motor skills

Equipment: 1 die (preferably numbered rather than dotted) and a simple game board, made by drawing six teddies onto a piece of paper or card. Onto each teddy's tummy draw the "spots" that you would find on the face of a die, from 1 to 6, in the correct pattern. You will also need counters in a different colour for each player. You can find a printable version of the game board at ActivityVillage.co.uk/teddy-bear-teddy-bear.

To play: Give each player a small pile of counters in one colour. Youngest child rolls first. He places his counter on the teddy with the corresponding number, then passes the die to the next player. If there is already a counter on the appropriate teddy, you miss your go. When all the teddies are covered, count up the counters. Whoever has placed the most counters is the winner.

Variations:

If you find teddy bears tricky to draw, copy our picture on the next page or try butterflies or fish instead! If you ask the children to colour in the picture and then laminate the boards you will be able to play the game over and over again.

Number Chicks

This game is similar to Teddy Bear, Teddy Bear, but Number Chicks concentrates on number recognition rather than on counting dots. There is also a fast and fun variation for older kids.

Age guide: 3+

Skills: Number recognition, counting, fine motor skills

Equipment: 1-3 dice. Make a game board by drawing six chicks onto a piece of paper or card, and numbering them 1 to 6. You can find a printable version of the game board at ActivityVillage.co.uk/number-chicks.

Younger children: Youngest child rolls first. He places his counter on the chick with the corresponding number, then passes the die to the next player. If there is already a counter on the appropriate chick, you miss your go. When all the chicks are covered, count up the counters to discover the winner.

Older children: This is a fast, two-player game. You will need a pile of about 10 counters for each player (in their own colour) as well as 2 dice (or try 3 dice for an even faster game).

The younger player starts by rolling the dice and placing a counter on the corresponding chicks. Each chick can hold a maximum of 2 of the same-coloured counters, at which points that chick is "held" for that player and the counters may not be moved or added to. If there is only one counter on a chick, it may be bumped off by the other player if he rolls the same number. Continue until all chicks are "held" by one or other player, then count to find the winner.

Balloons

There are a number of ways to play this game. It only takes a moment to draw up the "game board" but you can also find a link to a printable version below.

Age guide: 3+

Skills: Number recognition, Pencil control, (fine motor skills

Equipment: 1 die. A different colour pencil or crayon for each player. Draw six bunches of three balloons onto a piece of white card or paper, and number the balloons in each bunch with the same numbers from 1 to 6. So the balloons in the first bunch are all numbered 1, the balloons in the second bunch are all numbered 2 and so on. You can also find a printable version of the board here: ActivityVillage.co.uk/balloons-dice-game

Variation 1: Roll the die. Colour a balloon of the correct number. There are no winners or losers –just aim for a colourful picture! Try to have coloured at least one balloon of each number before stopping the game.

Variation 2: A competitive game! The first child to colour in three balloons with the same number wins. Be aware that there is often no winner in this game.

Variation 3: Play until one player has three full bunches of balloons coloured in (or for a certain length of time). This player is not necessarily the winner. Total up the score by adding the numbers on the coloured balloons. The winner has the highest score.

Variation 4: As Variation 3 above, but in this game if you already have a bunch of three balloons coloured in and throw the same number again, you must "pop" one of those balloons by crossing it out! That balloon no longer counts towards the final score.

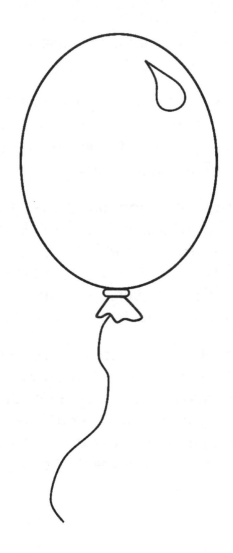

Beat That!

This is an easy game to learn, but one which is very popular with kids (and not too bad at keeping the odd grown up amused, too!). It is great for learning the concept of place value.

Age guide: 4+

Skills: Place value

Equipment: A minimum of 2 dice. You can use up to 7 dice for older players. Paper and pencil.

To play: Roll the dice and put them in order to make the highest number possible. If you roll a 4 and a 6, for example, your best answer would be 64. Using 3 dice, a roll of 3, 5 and 2 would give you 532, and so on.

If you are playing with younger children, it can be helpful to explain your reasoning out loud and encourage them to do the same.

Write down your answer, pass the dice, and challenge the next player to "Beat That!" Play in rounds and assign a winner to each round.

Variation:

Try making the smallest number possible!

Run For It!

This game is very quick and easy to learn, and is a good reinforcement of number sequencing for younger children.

Age guide: 4+

Skills: Sequences, counting, scoring (and the five times table)

Equipment: 6 dice, paper and pencil. For very young children you could play with numbered rather than dotted dice.

To play: Roll the dice and look for runs (sequences) starting with 1 (so 1-2, 1-2-3 and so on). Each dice which is part of a run scores five points. There can be more than one run in each roll.

A roll of 1-1-2-2-3-3 (with sequences of 1-2-3 and 1-2-3) would score 30.

A roll of 1-3-4-5-5-6 would score 0. Remember, sequences must *start* with a 1.

The first player to 100 points is the winner.

Mouse

This game may be familiar already - it is certainly an old favourite from my childhood. It can be enjoyed by any number and age of child and needs nothing but a scrap of paper, a pencil and a die.

Age guide: 5+

Skills: Number recognition, pencil control

Equipment: 1 die, pencil and paper for each player

To play: The aim of the game is to be the first to draw a complete Mouse. Take it in turns to roll once, then pass the die around. Each roll of the die enables a particular body part to be drawn as follows:

- 6 = body
- 5 = nose
- 4 = whiskers
- 3 = eyes
- 2 = ears
- 1 = tail

The body must be drawn before the other body parts are added to it, so players must roll a 6 to start. Once the body has been drawn, the other parts of the mouse may be added in any order. If you roll a number which relates to a part you have already added, you miss your go and pass the die on.

To play with younger children, draw a mouse lightly in pencil so that they can trace over the lines.

Beetle

Beetle is a well-known game very similar to Mouse, and just a little trickier.

Age guide: 5+

Skills: Number recognition, pencil control

Equipment: 1 die, pencil and paper for each player

To play: Beetle is played in the same way as Mouse. Roll one die and look at the number. If you have a 1 you can start by drawing the body. If not, pass the die to the next player.

- 1 = body
- 2 = head
- 3 = legs (3 legs per 3; you need 6 legs in total)
- 4 = eyes (one eye per 4)
- 5 = feelers (one feeler per 5)
- 6 = tail

Note that once you have a body you can make use of a 2, 3 or a 6 to draw head, legs and tail, but you won't yet be able to draw the eyes or feelers. As soon as one player has a complete Beetle the game is over.

Oh Dear!

A simple game, Oh Dear! was one of our family favourites when the kids were learning their numbers, but it's a game that children will enjoy any time, particularly the variation (which makes them giggle). You may want to make a colourful set of cards for each player but it only takes moments.

Age guide: 5+

Skills: Number recognition, fun

Equipment: 1 die (numbered for younger children), Six old playing cards Ace to 6, or six home-made cards numbered 1 to 6, for each player.

To play: Place the cards face up in a row in front of each player. Now players take turns to roll the die. Whatever number they roll, they turn the corresponding card face down. If they roll the same number again, they turn it face up again. The aim is to get all cards face down.

Variation (3 or more players):

This is more fun! Play is as above, but if your card is already face down when you roll a number, you can check the player on your left. If his card is still face up, turn it face down. Lucky him! If it is *already* face down, check the player on your right. If her card is still face up, turn it face down. Lucky her! If both players' cards are already face down, you have no choice but to turn your card face up again. Oh Dear!

Big Six

Although this has similarities to Oh Dear!, Big Six is a very different game. It's easy to learn and we have enjoyed playing this one. Apparently the game dates back to medieval times. The game is best with 2-6 players.

Age guide: 5+

Skills: Number recognition, fun

Equipment: 1 die, home-made game board (simply draw 6 boxes onto a piece of paper or card and number them 1 to 6), 5 counters given to each player

To play: The aim of the game is to be the first player to get rid of all your counters.

Roll the die and put a counter onto the corresponding numbered square. If there is already a counter on the square, you have to take that counter instead.

The exception is the box numbered six. Once a counter has been placed on it, it stays there until the end of the round. So rolls of six are a good way to get rid of your counters!

Higher or Lower

This game is based on a German dice game, also called Bouncer.

Age guide: 5+

Skills: Concept of higher and lower

Equipment: 1 die, 12 counters for each player

To play: Players aim to collect as many counters as possible – or rather, not to be thrown out of the game by owing more than they can pay!

Player 1 rolls the die and passes it to his left. Player 2 rolls and looks to see whether it is higher or lower. Whoever has the higher number pays the other the difference between the two numbers. Player 2 then passes the die to Player 3, who rolls, checks to see if it is higher or lower, and so on.

If you pay out all your remaining counters exactly in one turn, but not more, you have one more chance to stay in the game. If you should be paying out more counters than you have, you are thrown out. The game ends and the remaining playing count up for the winner.

Example Game:

Player 1 rolls 4.

Player 2 rolls 5 and collects 1 counter from Player 1.

Player 3 rolls 2 and gives 3 counters to Player 2.

Player 4 rolls 3 and collects 1 counter from Player 3.

And so on.

Variations:

For younger children, you may want to play with one numbered (rather than dotted) die *each* to help the children remember what the throws are and work out the "differences".

Going to Boston

This is a well-known game with easy rules, which is easily played by children.

Age guide: 5+

Skills: Addition

Equipment: 3 dice, paper and pencil

To play: Roll the dice and keep the highest die aside. Roll the remaining two dice and again set aside the highest. Roll the last die, and add up your total. Write down your score.

Play a number of rounds and then either total your points for the winner or simply count how many rounds were won by each player.

What's Your Number?

What's Your Number? can be enjoyed by all ages of children - and any number up to 6. It is an exciting and popular race game and is sure to become one of your favourites.

Age guide: 5+

Skills: Number recognition, pencil control

Equipment: 1-3 dice, paper and pencil for each player. Think up a simple picture that children can draw by themselves, or that you can draw for younger children to trace over, with a set number of lines. You could use, for example, a smiley face with 4 lines, a flower with 5 petals and a circular centre (6 lines), or a simple house like the one below with 12 lines. Agree your picture in advance and make sure the number of lines is appropriate for the age of the children playing.

To play: The youngest player rolls one dice and writes the number down. This is his special number. Each player then finds their own special number, rolling as many times as necessary to find one which has not been used by another player. If lots of children are playing, simply assign each one a number - it simplifies the process! You can also assign a child a number which they are currently learning or having difficulty with.

The player with the lowest number starts by rolling two dice. If your special number is rolled, you may add a line to your picture. It doesn't matter who actually rolls the dice; each player is allowed to fill in one of their lines if his or her number comes up, or two lines if a double is thrown. The first to complete their picture wins the game.

Variations:

Using one die throughout the game will slow it down; using three will speed it up!

You can play additional rounds and keep score by giving the winner the total of the lines left incomplete around the table. Or give everyone their own score of incomplete lines, and the overall winner is the one with the lowest total at the end of the game.

For a fast two or three player game, choose two numbers each.

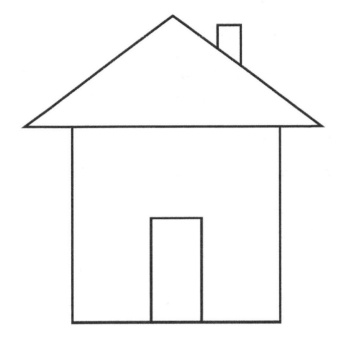

This house takes 12 "lines" to complete and makes a good picture for a 2-dice game.

Catch Up

This is a great game for groups of children and works with mixed ages well. You will need at least 4 children and up to 8 (any more than that and you should split them into two groups).

Age guide: 5+

Skills: Patience; rhythm and chanting

Equipment: 2 dice, 3 counters or small toys for each child

To play: The object of the game is to be the first to win 3 counters. The children sit in a circle around a table or on the floor. Split the dice so that the oldest child has one and the child sitting opposite has the other. Put the counters in the middle. The children who do not have the dice begin to create a rhythm by first slapping their knees (or the table) once and then clapping their hands once. When all children are synchronised they begin to chant as follows:

[Each section of the chant is marked by / and takes two beats]

/ Are you / ready? / Are you / ready? /

/ If ~ / so ~ / let's ~ / go! ~ /

/ Roll now! / *slap clap* / What have you got? / *slap clap* /

/ Must you pass? / *slap clap* / Hope not! / *slap clap* /

Repeat the chant over during play. At the "Roll now!" command, the children with the dice roll - hoping for anything but a 6! If it is 6, they must pass the die to the player on their left and take up the chant.

A child wins the round when he is still in possession of a die and is passed another from the child on his right. The winner of the round takes a counter. The first to collect 3 counters wins!

Variations:

For older children: Increase the speed of the chant for older children. Real professionals can begin to drop the extra / *slap clap* / for a very fast game indeed!

For big groups of children: If there are 6 or 8 children playing, you may wish to increase the passing roll to two numbers - say a 5 and a 6. This speeds the game up quite considerably.

Ten Down

It's possible to make a game out of basic maths drills, and this game does just that! As you are making your own dice, you can tailor this game precisely to the age and level of your child.

Age guide: 5+

Skills: Addition and subtraction

Equipment: 10 counters or small toys, 3 specially-prepared dice. To make the dice, use three blank dice or adapt existing dice with small stickers. On one of the die put 3 plus signs and 3 minus signs. On the other two dice, put the numbers 0 to 5.

To play: Put the 10 counters in a row in the middle of the players. The youngest starts and rolls all the dice, then works out the problem. You may need to remind younger children to put the largest number first in a subtraction problem. The answer to the sum is that player's score. Each player takes a turn and the winner of the round (the player with the highest score) takes a counter or toy from the middle. Play until all the counters have gone and count up to declare an overall winner.

Tip: Rather than using counters find a collection of 10 small toys which are close to your child's heart and rename the game to match. I used a much-loved collection of small trolls to create a rousing game of "Troll!" for my older child, and a little bundle of treasured possession (beads, pebbles etc) to create the game "Treasure!" for my younger child. We kept each game together in small drawstring bags and I adapted them as the children advanced.

Variations:

For older children: This game is easily adapted by changing the numbers on the dice or by using bought dice with 12 or 20 sides.

Times tables: Try practicing times tables by using two normal 6-sided dice or two 12-sided dice and multiplying the two numbers rolled. It's the competitive element that makes this fun!

Sevens

Sevens is a classic dice game that doesn't take too much strenuous thought!

Age guide: 5+

Skills: Addition, scoring

Equipment: 7 dice, paper and pencil

To play: The object of the game is to get the lowest score. Combinations of 7 (using any number of dice) score "0", and all other dice score their face value.

A new player starts each round. He rolls all seven dice and looks for combinations which add up to 7 He sets those combinations aside. He then gathers up any remaining dice and rolls again, again setting aside dice adding up to 7. He can choose to roll up to three times, but if he rolls less than three times the other players must match his number of rolls for the remainder of the round.

For example: the first player rolls 5-1-2-6-3-3-1 and sets aside the combinations 5-2, 6-1, and 3-3-1. He scores "0" and passes the dice to the next player, who only has one roll. He throws 5-2-6-6-2-2-2 and sets aside the combination 5-2, but then scores a terrifying 18 points. Great fun!

Mountain

Mountain is a well-known game which is called by many names, and apparently dates back to Roman times. Its simplicity makes it ideal for younger players, but with its variations it is popular with all ages.

Age guide: 5+

Skills: Number recognition, manipulating numbers, strategy (variations)

Equipment: 2-3 dice, paper and pencil. You can find Mountain printables here if you prefer: ActivityVillage.co.uk/mountain

To play: The object of the game is to be the first to climb your mountain, in number order, and then descend the other side.

Each player draws an inverted "v" to form a mountain on a piece of paper, and writes the numbers 1 through 5 up one side, a 6 at the top, and then numbers 5 through 1 down the other.

Allow the youngest player to start. He rolls two dice and hopes for a 1, which will allow him to cross the number 1 off his mountain. He must "ascend" in numerical order, so cannot cross off the 2 until he has crossed off the 1. If he rolls a 1 and a 2, however, he can cross both numbers off in one turn. Play continues until someone has made it all the way up their mountain and down the other side in the correct order.

Variations:

Introduce adding: For a quicker game, allow the players to add their dice together to produce another number. For example, a throw of 1 and 2 would allow that player to cross off the 1, the 2 and the 3, all in one turn.

Climb a higher mountain: If you decide to play by adding the dice together, it can be fun to increase the height of the mountain. Try 9, 10 or 12, but increase the number of dice to 3.

Random order: The character of the game can be changed by allowing players to cross off numbers in random order. However, all the numbers on the ascent must still be crossed off before a player can begin to descend the mountain. Play this variation with 3 dice and a mountain with numbers to 12. Each die may only be used once (but does not have to be used) in each go. This introduces a strategic element to the game. Children will soon realise that it is better to cross off the higher numbers first.

Martinetti: In this version of the game, use the numbers 1 to 12 and back to 1, and throw 3 dice. Allow each player to continue throwing until they can't move, and to add their dice together to form extra numbers. For example, if a player were to roll 1-2-4, he could cross off the numbers 1, 2, 3, 4, 5, 6 and 7 with that one roll! He might then roll 3-5-6 and cross off the 8. On his next roll he gets 2-3-3 and has to pass the dice to the next player.

Tip: You could draw a page of mountains and laminate it, then use a dry-wipe pen for repeat use.

Stuck in the Mud

This was one of our favourite family dice games when the kids were little. Children love the surprises that the game produces, with some turns ending abruptly and some going on for ever and ever!

Age guide: 6+

Skills: Mental addition and scoring.

Equipment: 5 dice, paper and pencil

To play: The aim of the game is to achieve the highest score. You can only score on a roll which does not include the numbers 2 and 5. Any dice which show a 2 or a 5 become "stuck in the mud".

Choose a player to start. Roll all 5 dice. If you have rolled any 2s or 5s, you do not score points for this throw. If you have not rolled any 2s or 5s, add up the total of the dice and remember it.

Set aside any 2s and 5s, and throw the remaining dice. Again, if you have rolled any

2s or 5s you fail to score this turn. Throws without 2s and 5s are added to your previous total.

Continue in this way until all your dice are "stuck". Write down your score, and pass the dice to the next player.

Agree a number of rounds (five works well) and total up the score. You may be surprised at just how tricky the dice can be!

Example Game:

Player 1 rolls 5, 2, 4, 4 3. She scores no points, and sets aside the 5 and 2. She rolls the remaining 3 dice and gets 6, 1, 4, totalling 11. She rolls 3 dice again, this time getting 2, 3, 4. She scores no points and sets aside the 2. She rolls 2 dice and gets 6, 6, scoring 12 to give a running total of 23. She rolls again for a 2 and a 3: no points. The last dice is a 5 so she is "stuck in the mud" with 23 points.

Player 2 rolls 1, 3, 4, 6, 6 and scores 20 points. He rolls the 5 dice again and gets 5, 5, 5, 3, 2. No points, and he has only 1 dice left to throw. He rolls for a 4 (24 points) and a 6 (30 points) and a 3 (33 points) and a 6 (39 points) before finally throwing a 5 and getting "stuck in the mud" for 39 points.

Player 3 rolls 2, 2, 5, 5, 5 and is stuck for 0!

Seven Up

Simple to learn and simple to play, this is a fun family game.

Age guide: 6+

Skills: Addition, subtraction

Equipment: 2 dice, about 20 counters for each player and 20 for the pot

To play: Roll the dice. If you throw 7, take 7 counters from the middle pot.

If you throw anything other than 7, work out the difference between the number you threw and 7, and put that number of counters in the pot.

Keep playing until someone loses all their counters. Then count up the remaining players' counters to see who won.

Example Game:

Player 1 rolls 2-4. He scores 6 and pays 1 counter into the pot.

Player 2 rolls 6-6. She scores 12 and pays 5 counters into the pot.

Player 3 rolls 3-4 and takes 7 counters from the pot.

Scratch

This is a simple game - in that it requires no complicated maths or painful strategic thinking - and as such is great for a group of mixed ages and abilities. But be warned: the frustration factor can be high and I found that by introducing either or both variations the traditional game was much improved.

Age guide: 6+

Skills: Patience!

Equipment: 2 dice, paper and pencil for each player

To play: Each game consists of 11 rounds, with each player trying to roll the number requested in each round and scoring that number of points if he does.

Each player starts by writing the numbers 2 through 12 in a row. Begin with the youngest player. The target for the first round is "2". Roll both dice and add them together. If you manage to reach the target (in this case achieved only by rolling a double 1) you can score "2". Circle the number. If you don't, "scratch" that number by putting a line through it. Pass the dice to the next player, who also tries to roll a 2 and either circles or scratches the number.

Play continues until all 11 rounds have been played, and the score sheet marked. Add the circled numbers to give each player's total (which will almost certainly be low) and declare a winner.

Children will quickly learn that the probability of hitting the lower and higher numbers is very low!

Variations:

Doubles: When you roll a double on your turn (and *don't* scratch the number with that throw) you can roll another time and try again. For example, if you rolled a double 3 on round 4, you could roll again.

Magic star: Cover over one of the one-spots on one of the dice with a little star sticker. If you roll that star you can use it as any number.

Three or More

I've included this game because it introduces a number of the concepts of more advanced dice games, and because it is well-known, not because I think it is a great game! We played it a few times and then moved on.

Age guide: 6+

Skills: Addition (scoring)

Equipment: 5 dice

To play: The object of the game is to get 3 or more of a kind. The more that you get, the more you score. The player with the highest score after a fixed number of rounds (5 works well) is the winner.

Roll the dice. You must have 2 of a kind to continue playing. If you don't, write "0" for your score for this round and pass the dice to the next player.

If you rolled 3, 4 or 5 of a kind on your first roll, score as below:

3 of a kind = 3 points

4 of a kind = 6 points

5 of a kind = 12 points

If you rolled only 2 of a kind, you have one more turn to improve your score. Put your 2 matching dice aside and roll the others again. If you succeed, score as above. If you don't, you get no score this turn.

Elevenses

This is similar to Seven Up, but probably more fun. If you roll an "Elevenses" you could be in for an exciting number of counters!

Age guide: 6+

Skills: Addition, subtraction

Equipment: 2 dice and 20 counters for each player plus 20 for the pot.

To play: Each player puts 2 counters into the centre at the beginning of their turn. They then roll the dice.

- If they roll a 12, they have to double the number of counters in the pot, if they can. If they can't, they should pay in as many as they can.
- If they roll an 11, they claim all the counters currently in the pot.
- If they roll less than 11, they have to pay the difference into the pot.

Play for a certain number of rounds, or until someone wins too many counters!

Jeopardy!

Jeopardy is fast and fun, and can be played by a crowd. It's great practice for quick mental addition, too. I found that the kids loved it when someone else rolled a 1 but not so much when they did!

Age guide: 6+

Skills: Addition, nerve!

Equipment: 1-2 dice, pencil and paper

To play: Each player aims to record the most points possible on his turn, with a target of 100 to win. Roll the die as long as you dare, adding up the total out loud as you go.

Stop at any time you like and write down your score because - and here is the jeopardy aspect – when you roll a 1 your turn is over and your score for that turn goes back to zero!

Variation:

Play with two dice and aim for 200. If you roll a double of any number apart from a double six, you lose your score for that turn.

Target

This must be the ultimate in portable games, with the only requirement being one die and some mental maths. Play the variations to keep the children on their toes!

Age guide: 6+

Skills: Addition and subtraction, mental maths

Equipment: 1-2 dice

To play: You are aiming for a target of 20, which you must hit exactly. The first player rolls the die and announces the number. The next player rolls and adds his/her number to the previous one.

Players take turns in this way, adding their number to the previous total. However, if by adding their number the total would be taken over 20, they must subtract their number instead. Continue until somebody hits the target!

Variations:

Target for more players: If there are more than 3 players, you may want to increase the target to 30.

Target 100: Target 100 is played in the same way, but two dice are used.

Countdown: This game is played in reverse. Start from 20 (or 100) and count down. Children (and adults) find this one much more difficult!

Odds and Evens

Odds and evens is pure luck. There is definitely adding and subtracting involved, but the addition of the counters in the stockpile disguises the maths and I've found that kids enjoy this game.

Age guide: 6+

Skills: Addition and subtraction

Equipment: 3-6 dice. 10 counters per player, placed in the centre of the table

To play: The object of the game is to have won the most counters from the stockpile in the centre of the table when the final counter is removed.

Roll all six dice. Add the even numbers together, and subtract the odd numbers. If you are left with a positive number, take that number of counters from the stockpile. If you are left with a negative number, you must pay that number into the stockpile (if you have any counters; if you don't, or don't have enough, just pay what you can). Play passes around the table until someone wins the last counter - at which point count up your counters and declare a winner.

Variations:

Play with 5 dice: 2 of one colour and 3 of the other. Subtract the total of the pair from the total of the other three dice.

Play with 3 dice: 1 of one colour and 2 of the other. Subtract the number of the single die from the total of the pair.

Par

This is another simple family game with an element of excitement to the scoring that keeps children coming back for more.

Age guide: 7+

Skills: Simple addition, simple strategy

Equipment: 5 dice, paper and pencil

To play: Agree a number of rounds (5 work well) and take turns to play. You are aiming to reach a total of at least 24 with all five dice.

Throw the dice and set aside at least one die, but as many as you wish. Pick up the remainder and throw again. You may throw as many times as you like, but you *must* set aside at least one more die for each throw.

Obviously if you throw a 6 you will set it aside; otherwise you will have to think about the target of 24 and how best to achieve it.

To score: If you throw less than 24, you score a negative number for how much you missed the target by. If you achieved only 20, you would score "minus 4".

If you throw exactly 24, you score "0".

If you throw more than 24, the number you exceed 24 by becomes your magic number.

A throw of 28, for example, would result in a magic number of 4. Write down 4 as your base score but then pick up all five dice and roll them. If any of the dice show your magic number, you can add them up as a bonus score. So a roll of 6-5-4-4-1 would give you a bonus score of 8 and a total score of 12.

Winner!

Traditionally known as "Multiplication" or "Multiply", a simple change of name has made this game very popular with our panel of testers who otherwise might have resisted this game!

Age guide: 6+

Skills: Addition, multiplication (times tables)

Equipment: 2 dice of one colour, 1 die of a different colour, pencil and paper

To play: Roll the three dice together. Add the two matching dice and then multiply the total by the third. Write down your score and pass the dice on.

Declare the player with the highest number the winner of the round. You can circle the winning score on your paper, or give the winner of each round a counter if you prefer.

Play 10 rounds in total, and then decide the overall winner.

Variations:

Play with four dice, two of one colour and two of another. Roll all four dice and add the pairs together, then multiply.

Play with one bought 12-sided die and one normal die, or with two 12-sided dice.

Meteor Shower

Meteor is a popular game which can be played with many variations to suit the ages and skills of the kids. Some children love the threat of the "meteor"; others, especially younger children, may be put off by it and prefer one of the toned down variations.

Age guide: 6+

Skills: Addition, mental maths

Equipment: 3 dice. For younger children you could cover the 1s with a small star sticker. Pencil and paper.

To play: The aim of the game is to be the first to reach 100 points. On each go, you roll the dice as follows and try to increase your score without meeting a meteor shower:

Roll all three dice and set aside the highest number. Roll the remaining two dice, and again choose the highest number. Roll the last dice, and then add the total of the three dice together. Keep a running total of your score and try to be the first to reach 100.

Disaster strikes if you meet a meteor shower - you go right back to zero again! A meteor shower occurs if on the first throw you roll three stars, on the second throw you roll two stars, or on the third throw you roll one star.

Variations:

Some children find the concept of going back to zero too daunting, and the game can go on a long time!

Try these ideas instead:

- You get no score at all for the throw which generated a meteor shower

- When you hit a meteor shower you take off 20 points (or go back to zero if you have less than 20 points).

- Create a simple game board, perhaps on the inside of a file folder or on a large piece of card. Put the Earth at one end and the Sun at the other. Make a path between the two using 90 plain spaces (white stickers work well) and 8 "planets" or stars. Using playing pieces, start on the Earth and aim for the Sun. When you hit a meteor shower, fall back to the last planet or star.

House Numbers

This game is a more advanced version of Beat That! It is great for reinforcing place value and also involves an element of strategic thinking.

Age guide: 6+

Skills: Place value, strategy

Equipment: 1 die, paper and pencil for each player

To play: The aim of House Numbers is to allocate the numbers you roll to give your "street" the highest overall score. Each player should draw a "street" of three simple houses, each of which should have three boxes in front for the house number. Older children can simply draw three boxes, each divided into three, or a square with three rows and three columns.

Play goes as follows: Roll the die and decide which box of which house you will write the number into. You will obviously want to put the lower numbers into "unit" positions and the higher numbers into "hundred" positions.

Take it in turns to write in a number and then pass the dice. When all the boxes are filled, total up your score, adding all three house numbers together, to find the winner.

If you play more than one game, allow a different player to start each time. The later players have an advantage by being able to see what numbers they will need to beat; this allows them to take fewer risks with their throws.

Shut the Box

Shut the box is a very well-known old game, most commonly seen now as wooden "parlour" game with a felt-lined box. It works fine with paper and pencil, though, and is a good way to introduce strategic thinking to children.

Age guide: 6+

Skills: Strategy

Equipment: 2 dice, paper and pencil or a simple home-made "game board" and 9 counters.

For a paper and pencil game: Write the numbers 1 to 9 in a row.

To make a simple game board: Draw a square and divide it into three rows and three columns to give you 9 squares (big enough to hold your counters). Number the squares 1 to 9 starting at the top left and working along the rows.

To make a more permanent game board: Use a shallow box and its lid. Mark out the game board in the bottom of the box and use the lid for rolling the dice. Keep the counters and dice in the box.

To play: Throw the dice and mark off (or place a counter on) either the two numbers thrown, or the box which corresponds to their total. Note that if you throw a double 6 or a double 5, you are instantly out of the game!

Keep rolling and crossing numbers off (or placing counters over the numbers) until you cannot go. Add up the remaining numbers on your board and pass the dice to the next player. The player with the lowest score at the end of the round wins.

There is one more important rule. Once the numbers 7, 8 and 9 have been marked off, a player may continue with only one die if she wishes.

Variations:

An easier game: For a slightly easier and longer game, you can allow the players to mark off any combination of numbers which produce the same total as the total on their dice. So a throw of a 6 and a 5, totalling 11, could also be played with the 8 and the 3, or the 8, the 2 and the 1, and so on. In this game the best strategy is to mark off the higher numbers first.

Solitaire: Shut the Box can be a good solitaire game. Simply try to mark off all the numbers, or "Shut the Box".

Tower

Tower is relatively simple to learn and enjoy but we have found that younger children find it hard to avoid knocking down the towers by accident (or on purpose!).You need at least 3 to play, and the game is better with more.

Age guide: 7+

Skills: Strategy

Equipment: 6 dice per player in their own colour, paper and pencil for scoring

To play: One player gathers up all the dice and rolls them in the centre of the table. Try to keep them a little contained! The player to his or her left begins play.

The aim is to claim as many towers as possible. Towers consist of a stack of more than one die of the same number, but there can be no more than 3 dice in a tower. The stack is claimed by the player with the dice on top.

Player 1 looks to see if she can start building a tower by finding another player's die with the same number as her own. She simply places her matching die on top. If she can build, she must. You cannot build onto your own dice.

Play passes to the left, with each player building if they can. Once a tower has 3 dice in it, that tower is "claimed" and cannot be built on further, nor can the dice within it be removed.

If it is your turn and you can't build, you may select one of your free dice and roll it once. If you can then build, do so immediately. If you cannot build, you miss that go.

Play continues until one player has built with his last dice. At this point each player is allowed one more turn only. This can happen quite quickly and unexpectedly.

Scoring: Score 15 for each tower of 3 dice; score 10 for each tower of 2 dice. Play a fixed number of rounds (5 works well) and then total the scores for the overall winner.

Variations:

In a three player game you may decide to allow the players to build onto their own dice.

Bank

If you love arithmetic, this is the game for you. And if you don't, you are certainly going to get better at it if you play this game a few times! This is a fun way to get children adding, subtracting, multiplying and dividing.

Age guide: 8+

Skills: Arithmetic

Equipment: 1 die, paper and pencil

To play: Roll the die five times in a row. You must add the first two numbers and subtract the third. If the answer at that stage is zero or less, your turn is over and you record a score of zero.

If you have a positive number, you continue by multiplying by the fourth number and dividing by the fifth. Ignoring remainders, write down your score and pass the die to the next player.

After four rounds, total your scores. The winner has the highest total.

Banker

This is a more difficult variation of Bank which is perfect for honing arithmetic skills as well as developing strategic thinking. Note the variations, which can change Banker into a speed game too.

Age guide: 8+

Skills: Arithmetic, strategy

Equipment: 1 die, paper and pencil

To play: The aim of the game is to get the highest possible score in each of the rounds, and the highest overall score. As in the previous game, each player rolls the die five times. In this game he chooses the operations he wishes to use – adding, subtracting, multiplying or dividing - using each only once and basing his decision as best he can on the numbers he has thrown.

Once again you should play four rounds and total up to find the highest score.

Variations:

All at once: Play with five dice and roll them all at once. Decide how best to use the operations to reach the highest score.

Beat the teacher: One person (perhaps the teacher or an adult) rolls five dice without showing the others and works out the highest score that can be achieved. The dice are then revealed and the other players race to be the first to work out how to achieve that number.

Beat the clock: Five dice are rolled and placed so that all players can see them (or written up on the blackboard in a classroom situation). The players race against the clock to find the highest score. You could start with 2 minutes on the clock and then reduce it according to the ability of the players.

Target 23

This is a simple game but one which can be played quietly with two players or noisily with a whole classroom of kids. And it is great practice for manipulating numbers and getting the brain working harder.

Age guide: 8+

Skills: Arithmetic

Equipment: 4 dice, paper and pencil for each player, a timer (optional)

To play: The aim of Target 23 is to make the number 23 (or as close as possible to 23) with a roll of four dice. You may use any of the four operations - add, subtract, multiply or divide - and you may use each one as many times as you like. You MUST use each die, and you must use each die only ONCE.

If you are playing with a small number of players, we suggest you give each player a paper and pencil and roll the dice in the middle of the table so that everyone can see them. With a bigger group (or in the classroom), one player can roll the dice and then call out the numbers to be written down by each player.

Target 23 works best if you have a timer or stopwatch to add some pace and excitement to the game. When all players can see the numbers (or they have been written down on their paper), set the timer to (say) 2 minutes. The first player to work out a way of reaching the target exactly can call "Target 23!" The other players continue to try to reach the target for the allotted length of time. When the time is up, the first player's result is checked, and, if correct, he is awarded a bonus of 3 points. All other players who reached the target score 1 point. Players who did not reach the target score zero!

Obviously it will not always be possible to reach the target. In this case when the time is up the players say how close they managed to get to 23. If their total is within 3 points either side of 23, they score 1 point.

Play a fixed number of rounds - five works well - and then total up the scores.

Go!

There is absolutely no skill involved in this game apart from speed but really is a great, noisy party game (although you can also play with just 2) and is a fun ice-breaker or mixer when you have multiple generations. You will need lots of dice! Many different ways of playing make this a really good, fun game.

Age guide: 8+

Skills: Speed

Equipment: 6-12 dice in one colour for each player, the more the better. You can also give each player the lid of a shoe box to play in, in which case it doesn't matter if their dice don't match.

To play: One player shouts "Go!" and everyone frantically rolls their dice until they have a complete set of one number, at which they shout loudly that they have won!

Variations:

It's fun to play "Go!" in rounds, giving the winner of each round the chance to choose what happens in the next. Some ideas are:

- The previous winner shouts "Go 4!" (or another number of his choice) and everyone must roll that number.

- The previous winner rolls his dice, looks at them, and then calls out the number that everyone must roll.

- The previous winner shouts "Sequence!" at the start of the round. All players must try to get 1-2-3-4-5-6 if they are playing with 6 dice, or an agreed variation according to the number of dice you are playing with (for example, 1-2-3-4-5-5-4-3-2-1 if you are playing with 10 dice).

- The previous winner calls "Totals!" and the players roll all their dice and then race to add up their dice first. Check

that the winner reached the correct
total!

- The previous winner calls "Pairs!" and
all dice must be matched up in
different pairs.

I'm sure that the kids can come up with more
ideas!

Bluff

Bluff – and the next two games, Liar Dice and Dudo, are played in various forms all over the world. Bluff is the simplest and can be played with 3-5 players. I personally think that the variation works better as a game, but it is harder for younger children to grasp.

Age guide: 8+

Skills: Addition, poker face, strategy

Equipment: 3 dice and a dice cup or plastic mug. Five counters for each player.

To play: The aim of the game is to get rid of all your counters first. Player 1 uses the dice cup to roll all three dice, keeping them hidden. He peeks, adds up the total of the dice, and then announces a total – any total he chooses, not necessarily the actual total – to the player on his left.

Player 2 decides whether he believes Player 1's "call". If he does, he "accepts" the dice, which are passed around carefully still underneath the dice cup. Make sure that the children understand that the dice shouldn't be rolled as they are moved!

As soon as Player 2 "accepts", Player 1 puts one counter into the "pot" (the centre of the table) as reward for a successful call. If Player 2 doesn't accept the call, he can say "Bluff!" in which case Player 1 has to show the dice. If the dice were the same as, or greater than the total (that is, the call was correct), he can give away a counter to Player 2. If they were less than he called (that is, he was Bluffing), Player 2 gives away a counter to him.

If Player 2 decided to accept the call, he now has to roll the dice again and pass them on to Player 3, *calling a higher number than the one he accepted*. The dice continue around the table, increasing with every call and with a counter put into the centre with each successful pass, until someone again calls "Bluff!"

Children will soon learn to start with a low call, or the dice will come back round the table and bite them!

Example Game, with 4 players:

Player 1 rolls 2-4-6. He calls "8" and passes the dice.

Player 2 accepts, and rolls 4-5-6. He calls "15" and passes the dice.

Player 3 accepts. He rolls 1-2-4 and calls "16" and passes the dice.

Player 4 calls Bluff, and gives away a counter to Player 3.

Player 4 now starts the next round.

Variation:

When you accept a call and receive the dice cup, you don't have to re-roll all – or any – of the dice. Look, choose whether you want to keep any of the dice, and carefully roll the others so that the other players can't see the result. Place all three dice back under the cup and state your "call". This variation is better for older children, and I think it makes a better game.

Liar Dice

Liar Dice is a harder version of Bluff, for which children will have to learn some of the poker hands.

Age guide: 10+

Skills: Poker hands, poker face, bluffing, strategy

Equipment: 5 dice and a dice cup or plastic mug. Five counters for each player.

To play: As with Bluff, the aim of the game is to get rid of all your counters first.

Player 1 rolls all five dice under the dice cup, and makes a call according to the following poker hands (ranked lowest to highest):

- High number
- One pair
- Two pairs
- Three of a kind
- Low straight (1-2-3-4-5)
- High straight (2-3-4-5-6)
- Full house (Three of a kind + one pair)

- Four of a kind
- Five of a kind (obviously this isn't possible in poker!)

Play continues as in Bluff. Player 2 needs to decide whether to accept the call, in which case he is going to have to beat it on his turn – or call "Liar!" and challenge Player 1 to reveal the dice. Once the call is accepted, Player 1 can give away a counter and breathe a sigh of relief!

Player 2, having accepted the call, can now look at the dice and decide to roll any or all of them again, secretly, before making his call and trying to pass the dice around.

Example Game, with 4 players:

Player 1 rolls 1-2-3-3-4 and calls "pair of 3s"

Player 2 sets aside the 3s (keeping them hidden) and rolls the other dice, getting 1-4-5. He calls "pair of 4s" (a bluff).

Player 3 therefore receives 1-3-3-4-5. She rolls the 1-4-5 and gets 1-2-6, and decides to call "two pairs, 1s and 3s" (a bluff).

Player 4 receives 1-2-3-3-6 and rolls the 1-2-6 again, getting 3-6-6. Player 4 calls "Full House".

Player 1 has to decide whether to accept Full House – which seems a possible result given the previous call of 2 pairs – or to call Liar. If he accepts he has no choice but to call "Four of a Kind" or even "Five of a Kind" on his turn, so he decides it is better to call Liar instead. He loses the call and has to take a counter from Player 4.

Dudo

Dudo is a very old game which has also been packaged up with a slightly different name for sale. It is popular with older children and adults too. Dudo is Spanish for "I doubt".

Age guide: 10+

Skills: Bluffing, poker face, strategy

Equipment: 5 dice and a dice cup or plastic mug for each player.

To play: The aim of Dudo is to be the last player left in the game, by counting and calculating dice possibilities, reading the other players to guess when they are bluffing, and having a bit of luck!

In Dudo, a 1 is known as an Ace and is a "wild" die.

Each player starts with a dice cup and 5 dice. Choose the first player however you like, and then work clockwise around the table.

On Player 1's signal, everyone shakes their dice onto the table, keeping them hidden under their cup, and looks carefully at what they have without letting the other players see their dice.

Player 1 thinks about the possible dice combinations on the table and makes a "call" based on the total number of dice on the table. He should bear in mind that 1s can be wild (which makes higher numbers more likely), that the number of dice in play varies throughout the game, and that the first "call" in each round cannot be Aces. An opening call might be "six 3s".

Player 2 can now choose to accept the call and make a higher call (see below), or to challenge the previous player by calling Dudo.

Remember, players can bluff at any time!

Making a higher call:

Option 1: Player 2 can call the same number of dice but increase the dot value. For example, if Player 1 called "six 3s", Player 2 could increase that by calling "six 4s".

Option 2: He can call a higher number of dice with the same dot value. For example, if Player 1 called "six 3s", Player 2 could increase that by calling "seven 3s".

Option 3: He could make a call with Aces, which is at least half of the number of the previous call. For example, if Player 1 called "six 3s", Player 2 could increase that by calling "three Aces".

Further into the game, you can change a call in Aces back to any other dot value as long as you call at least double the number of Aces plus 1. So a call of "three Aces" could be increased by calling "seven 2s" or any other dot value.

Calling Dudo:

When it is her turn, if a player believes that the previous call is too high, she may call Dudo. Everyone lifts their cup and reveals their dice, and they are counted up to see whether the call was good or not. If the call was good, the challenger loses a die. If the call was bad, the caller loses a die. The lost die is put to one side.

NB: Traditionally the lost die is hidden away so that the players have to remember the number of dice on the table for each round. If you are playing with younger children you might want to keep the counters visible.

Example Dudo Round:

There are 4 players, giving a total of 20 dice.

Player 1 rolls 2, 2, 3, 3, 4. He calls "six 2s."

Player 2 rolls 1, 2, 2, 4, 6. He calls "seven 2s."

Player 3 rolls 1, 1, 3, 4, 5. As she has no 2s herself she doesn't want to increase the call to "eight 2's". She has Aces, however, and thinks a low call will be safe. She calls "four Aces."

Player 4 rolls 1, 2, 5, 6, 6. She calls "nine 2s".

Player 1 thinks. He knows he has two 2s only. He thinks that Player 2 has at least one 2 and suspects that Player 3 has no 2s but at least two Aces. He thinks Player 4 must also have 2s. He is reluctant to increase the call to "ten 2s" and debates changing it instead to "nine

3s". In the end he loses confidence and instead calls "Dudo".

When all the dice are counted up, there are a total of five 2s but with the additional four "wild" Aces the declared total is "nine 2s". Player 1 has lost the challenge and has to hand in one die.

Continuing Play:

The loser of the first round starts the next, and play continues until one player has only one die left. The rules then change as follows.

Palifico:

The player with only one die remaining announces that he is "palifico". He starts the next round, even if it was someone else's turn. In a palifico round, Aces are no longer "wild" and the only way to increase the *opening* call is to increase the number of dice. For the rest of the round, only "palifico" players are allowed to change the number. Towards the end of the game there may be several players who are "palifico".

About the Author

Lindsay Small is the creator and owner of www.ActivityVillage.co.uk, a UK website which has helped parents, grandparents and teachers keep kids busy since 2000, with thousands of free colouring pages, puzzles, worksheets and printable activities as well as an enormous collection of craft ideas and games. Activity Village has well over a million visitors each month.

More Books by Lindsay Small:

Card Games for Kids

Superstar Sudoku for Kids

Superstar Sudoku for Kids on the Go

Made in the USA
Monee, IL
15 December 2022